THIS WALKER BOOK BELONGS TO:

For Matthew and Joe
S.H.

For Barbara
J.W.

First published 1988
by Walker Books Ltd
87 Vauxhall Walk
London SE11 5HJ

This edition published 1989

Printed in Italy by Grafedit S.p.A.

British Library Cataloguing in Publication Data
Hayes, Sarah
The Boot gang's Christmas caper.
I. Title II. Wijngaard, Juan
823'.914[J] PZ7
ISBN 0-7445-1329-4

written by
SARAH HAYES

illustrated by
JUAN WIJNGAARD

WALKER BOOKS
LONDON

Annie Boot was a burglar. Her father had been a burglar, and so had her grandfather. And when Annie Boot had twin boys, they turned out to be burglars too.

When he was little, Jojo Boot was good at climbing trees and balancing on washing lines. Annie hoped that he might grow up to be a big star in the circus. But Jojo became a burglar instead.

Bubbles Boot loved to take apart old clocks and radios, and he was very clever at making working models out of bits and pieces. Annie thought that Bubbles might grow up to be an engineer, or even an inventor. But Bubbles became a burglar like his brother.

The Boots were well known to the police, and they were on Wanted posters all over town. But the Boot Gang had never been caught: the fact is that Annie Boot was a master of disguise. No one ever recognised her or Jojo or Bubbles, not on the beach, nor in the theatre, nor at the museum, nor at football matches or garden fêtes or civic parades.

But everyone knew when the Boot Gang had been at work.

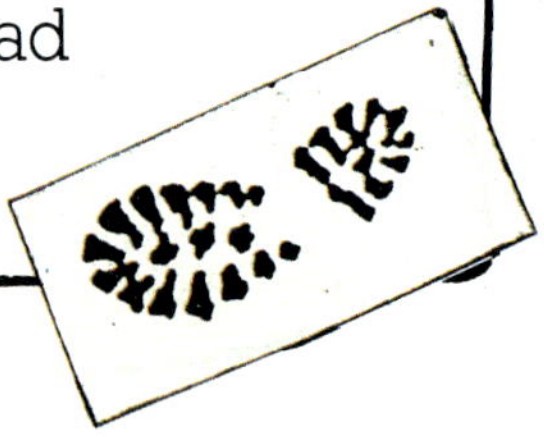

Of all their disguises, Annie's favourite was the one they used only once a year, for the great Christmas Caper. The false beard made Annie sneeze and Jojo found the sledge heavy going. Bubbles complained about always having to be the back end. But as a disguise it worked beautifully.

If people looked out of their windows and saw a reindeer waiting patiently under the lamplight, they smiled to themselves and drew their curtains.

If children woke in the night to find a person in red beside their beds, they quickly closed their eyes and turned over.

If there seemed to be odd thuds on the roof and sneezings in the chimney, no one paid any attention – not on Christmas Eve.

Every year Annie and Jojo and Bubbles stole presents from under trees, from bottom drawers and the tops of wardrobes, and even out of stockings and pillowcases.

When they got home, the Boots made three huge piles of presents and unwrapped them. Jojo and Bubbles didn't always get what they wanted, but Annie was always delighted.

"That'll come in handy," she'd say, and it always did. Of course the Boots didn't bother giving each other presents, but nobody minded that.

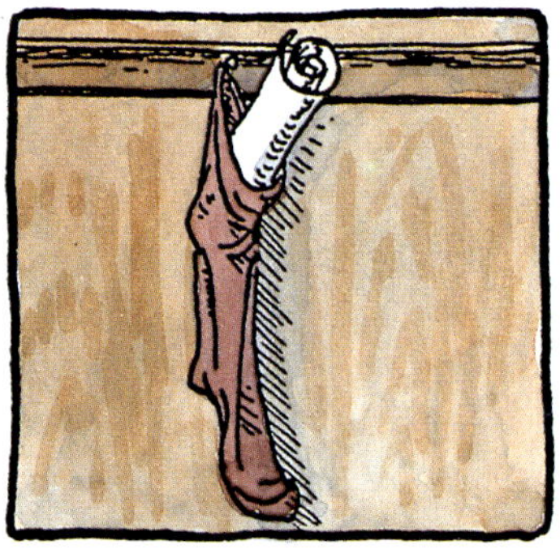

Eventually the Boot Gang became so rich that they decided to give up burgling and retire.

"We could lie on the beach sometimes," said Jojo. "I could learn to swim."

"We could go to the opera," said Annie.

"And drive out to the country," said Bubbles.

"There will be one last Christmas Caper," said Annie, "and it will be the best ever."

The Boot Gang set to work at once. Bubbles designed a power-assisted sledge. Jojo taught Annie to walk along roof ridges and come down chimneys without making a sound. Annie created an improved reindeer costume which didn't sag in the middle and had a truly magnificent set of antlers. And she made herself a new false beard which didn't tickle her nose and make her sneeze.

The Boots studied maps and made elaborate plans. They practised split-second timing with Annie's stopwatches. Jojo and Bubbles put on their reindeer costume and taught themselves to trot and gallop and even to jump over small obstacles. It was going to be the best Christmas Caper ever, and nothing could possibly go wrong.

BURGLAR OF THE YEAR CUP
IT ONLY HURTS WHEN I GO HO, HO, HO
CHEEKY
YOU'LL HAVE TO LOSE SOME WEIGHT MUM
THE BOOT HOUSE CLEARANCE COMPANY
PRIDE

Annie usually picked parts of the town where rich people lived, because they had the biggest, most expensive presents. This year she chose Willow Walk, because that was where the richest people of all lived.

On Christmas Eve the weather was perfect. The snow had stopped, and there was just enough moon to light up the roof-tops.

"Look at all those stars," said Bubbles, but Annie told him to be quiet and get into the back of the reindeer.

All went exactly as they had planned. The runners of the new, power-assisted sledge slid smoothly along the snow-covered roads, and the improved reindeer trotted

elegantly in front, lifting its feet and pointing its hooves. No one heard sneezings in the chimneys of Willow Walk. And only a sprinkling of soot dropped into the grates as Annie slipped into house after house and left with her sack by way of the front door.

At the end of Willow Walk stood a funny little house quite different from the rest. Annie didn't remember ever having seen it before. She decided not to bother with it. Then Jojo looked through the window and gasped.

"Look at that!" he whispered to Bubbles.

"Look at what?" said Bubbles crossly. He couldn't see anything from the back end of the reindeer.

Just then Annie came out of the house next door. She looked through the window of the funny little house and gasped, just like Jojo. There was the tallest Christmas tree and the biggest pile of presents Annie had ever seen in her life.

"We've got to have some of those," said Jojo, and Annie agreed.

The chimney of the funny little house was narrow and dirty, and Annie got covered in soot. But she soon found the room with the tall Christmas tree and the enormous pile of presents. She had almost filled her sack when she heard a cough behind her.

"Ho-ho-ho," said Annie gruffly, which was what she usually said if anyone saw her.

"And a ho-ho-ho to you," said someone in a very deep voice.

Annie started. This wasn't what usually happened, not at all. She turned round, gave a little scream, and dropped her sack. Standing in front of her was a person in red with a huge white beard and big black boots; someone who looked very like Annie herself.

"You're not..." quavered Annie. "You're not the real..." Annie's voice trailed off into silence.

"Ho-ho-ho," the person in red said again.

Annie pulled herself together. She strode across the room and gave a tug on the huge white beard.

"Ouch!" said the person in red. Then Annie did something she had never done before. She fainted dead away.

"That's what comes of taking other people's presents, Annie Boot," said Father Christmas. He picked Annie off the floor and put her gently down in a soft armchair. Then he shouldered his sack and vanished up the chimney.

In the street outside Jojo and Bubbles were also in trouble. One minute Jojo was half asleep and dreaming about the huge pile of presents. And the next, something started to woofle at him. Then something else stamped on his foot. Jojo opened his eyes and shut them again very quickly. Crowding curiously around him and Bubbles, and all woofling and stamping in the cold air, were eight enormous reindeer.

Jojo panicked. He put down his antlers and tried to charge off at full gallop. Bubbles had no idea what was happening and he tried to trot elegantly. As a result the twins got absolutely nowhere and fell in a tangled heap on the snow. The two halves of the reindeer came apart with a horrible tearing sound.

Out of the darkness above the roof-tops came a long, low whistle. The eight reindeer pricked up their ears, and with a great whooshing noise, they took off into the air and disappeared.

Two policemen coming round the corner of Willow Walk heard the whistle.

"Something's going on," said one of the policemen. They hurried towards the noise and ran straight into the heap of struggling Boots.

"It's our lucky night," said the policemen as they marched the Boot Gang towards the police station. Annie and Jojo and Bubbles said nothing. They looked white and very shaken.

The Boot Gang spent Christmas in prison that year, and the next, and several more after that. They never spoke about what had happened on the last Christmas Caper.

Eventually the time came for the Boots to leave prison. They were going to be released on New Year's Day, and they could hardly wait for Christmas to be over. On Christmas morning, however, Jojo woke up to find a present on the end of his bunk. "For Jojo Boot," said the label.

"I've never had a present specially for me," shouted Jojo. "Who sent it?" But no one seemed to know. Annie and Bubbles had presents on their beds too.

Jojo tore open the wrappings, and found a pair of armbands, some sunglasses and a shirt with palm trees on it. Bubbles had a set of spanners and a pair of bright blue overalls. Annie had a ticket for the opera and some very sharp cutting shears.

ROYAL OPERA
HOUSE
ADMIT ONE

And when they came out of prison the Boot Gang stopped being burglars. Jojo learned to swim and became a lifeguard. Bubbles joined a garage which repaired old sports cars. And Annie got a job making costumes for the theatre. They were very busy and very happy. Every Christmas the Boots gave each other presents, and they always got exactly what they wanted.

One day, quite by chance, Annie found herself in Willow Walk. She hurried past all the grand houses, glancing occasionally to left and right. It was a curious thing, but she just couldn't seem to find the funny little house at the end of the row. Just as well, Annie thought, and she caught the bus back to work.

The Boots never found out who had sent them the mysterious presents in prison. But once in a while Jojo or Bubbles would hear a long, low whistle above the roof-tops on Christmas Eve. And Annie would think back to the very last Christmas Caper. "Never again," she would say, and shake her head. And sometimes, very, very occasionally, she would catch the faint sound of a "ho-ho-ho" in the chimney.

MORE WALKER PAPERBACKS

PICTURE BOOKS
For the very young

Helen Oxenbury
Pippo

No.1 TOM & PIPPO READ A STORY
No.2 TOM & PIPPO MAKE A MESS
No.3 TOM & PIPPO GO FOR A WALK
No.4 TOM & PIPPO AND THE WASHING MACHINE
No.5 TOM & PIPPO GO SHOPPING
No.6 TOM & PIPPO'S DAY
No.7 TOM & PIPPO IN THE GARDEN
No.8 TOM & PIPPO SEE THE MOON
No.9 TOM & PIPPO AND THE DOG
No.10 TOM & PIPPO IN THE SNOW
No.11 TOM & PIPPO MAKE A FRIEND
No.12 PIPPO GETS LOST

Niki Daly
Story time

LOOK AT ME! JUST LIKE ARCHIE
MONSTERS ARE LIKE THAT
BEN'S GINGERBREAD MAN
TEDDY'S EAR
THANK YOU HENRIETTA

Sarah Hayes & Jan Ormerod
HAPPY CHRISTMAS, GEMMA
EAT UP, GEMMA

Sarah Hayes & Toni Goffe
CLAP YOUR HANDS
STAMP YOUR FEET

Ron Maris
IN MY GARDEN

Nicola Bayley
NONSENSE RHYMES

FIRST READERS

Allan Ahlberg & Colin McNaughton
Red Nose Readers

MAKE A FACE SO CAN I
BIG BAD PIG BEAR'S BIRTHDAY
SHIRLEY'S SHOPS PUSH THE DOG
TELL US A STORY ONE, TWO, FLEA!

Colin West
"HAVE YOU SEEN THE CROCODILE?"
"HELLO GREAT BIG BULLFROG"
"PARDON?" SAID THE GIRAFFE
"NOT ME SAID," THE MONKEY

Colin & Jacqui Hawkins
TERRIBLE TERRIBLE TIGER
THE WIZARD'S CAT

Chris Riddell
BEN AND THE BEAR
THE FIBBS

Penny Dale
BET YOU CAN'T

Sarah Hayes & Helen Craig
THIS IS THE BEAR
THIS IS THE BEAR AND THE PICNIC LUNCH

David Lloyd & Charlotte Voake
DUCK

PICTURE BOOKS
For 4 to 6-Year-Olds

Philippe Dupasquier
ROBERT THE GREAT
ROBERT THE PILOT
THE GREAT ESCAPE

Helen Craig
Susie and Alfred

THE NIGHT OF THE PAPER BAG MONSTERS
THE KNIGHT, THE PRINCESS AND THE DRAGON

Martin Waddell & Patrick Benson
THE TOUGH PRINCESS

Martin Handford
WHERE'S WALLY?
WHERE'S WALLY NOW?

PICTURE BOOKS
For 6 to 10-Year-Olds

Colin McNaughton
THE RAT RACE
SANTA CLAUS IS SUPERMAN
THERE'S AN AWFUL LOT OF WEIRDOS IN OUR NEIGHBOURHOOD

David Lloyd & Charlotte Voake
THE RIDICULOUS STORY OF GAMMER GURTON'S NEEDLE

E. J. Taylor
Biscuit, Buttons and Pickles

IVY COTTAGE THE THORN WITCH
GOOSE EGGS RAG DOLL PRESS